DISNEY

CLUB PENGUIN™

Waddle Lot of Laughs
Joke Book

Published by Ladybird Books Ltd 2009
A Penguin Company

Penguin Books Ltd, 80 Strand,
London, WC2R ORL, UK
Penguin Books Australia Ltd,
Camberwell, Victoria, Australia
Penguin Group (NZ), 67 Apollo Drive, Rosedale, North
Shore 0632, New Zealand
(a division of Pearson New Zealand Ltd)

www.ladybird.com
ISBN:9781409302988

13

Printed in Great Britain

Waddle Lot of Laughs
Joke Book

by Rebecca McCarthy

Which Way to Club Penguin?

TOURS

Once there were three penguins, Len, Ken and Pip, who decided to have a competition. While on top of a hill, each penguin had to throw his watch in the air, then run down the hill and catch it before it hit the ground.

First, Len threw his watch in the air, ran down the hill and *SPLAT*! The watch hit the ground. He wasn't fast enough.

Then, Ken threw his watch in the air and ran down the hill, but *SPLAT*! His watch hit the ground because he wasn't fast enough, either.

Finally, Pip threw his watch in the air, ran down the hill, went over to the Plaza for a slice of pizza, did some shopping over at the Sport Shop, went ice skating at the Ice Rink, played in the Snow Forts, had a cup of coffee in town and then came back and caught his watch.

"How did you do that?" asked the other two penguins.

Pip replied, "My watch is one hour slow."

Around Town

Pip walked into town with a lump of gravel under his arm. He asked another penguin if he could recommend a good place to get some refreshments.

The penguin said, "Sure, there are a couple of places on Club Penguin to get a drink. What were you looking for exactly?"

Pip considered the lump of gravel under his arm and said, "Oh, nothing fancy — just one bottle of soda for me and one for the road."

Q: What's black and white and red all over?

A: A blushing penguin.

Q: What's a penguin's favourite time at school?

A: Frost grade.

Q: Why did the penguin sniffle and cry on February 29th?

A: It was weep year.

Q: What do you call a penguin's shiny bill?

A: A sleek beak.

Q: What do penguins wear on their feet when they visit Holland?

A: Wooden shoe like to know?

Q: Who's a penguin's favourite aunt?

A: Aunt Arctic.

Q: Where can a penguin wander around aimlessly?

A: Rome.

Q: Where is a penguin most likely to slip and fall?

A: Greece.

Q: Where can a penguin go to borrow money?

A: Barce-loan-a.

Q: Why don't you see penguins in Britain?

A: Because they're afraid of Wales.

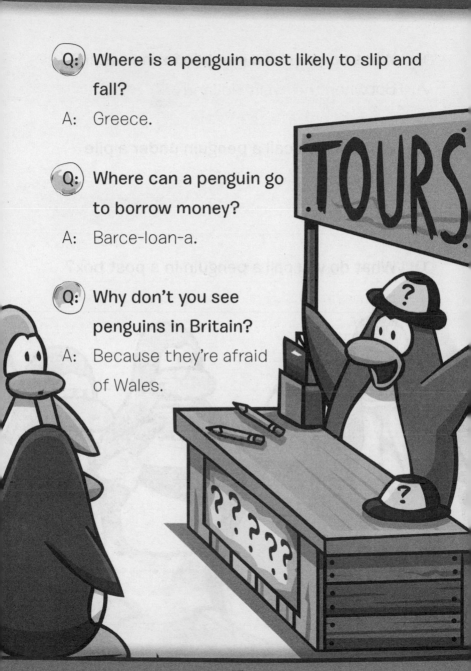

Q: What do you call a penguin in the water?

A: Bob.

Q: What do you call a penguin under a pile of leaves?

A: Russell.

Q: What do you call a penguin in a post box?

A: Bill.

DAN: Do you have holes in your socks?

HAL: I most certainly do not!

DAN: Then how do you get your feet into them?

AMY: I know a penguin with a wooden wing named Jim.

BOB: What's the name of his other wing?

ALI: I think I'm going to go inside the changing rooms at the Gift Shop to throw a temper tantrum.

ZAK: Why inside the changing rooms?

ALI: Isn't that a good place for fits?

Snow Fort Funnies

Lin wandered into the Snow Forts late one afternoon and came upon a group of penguins huddled behind a snow fort. Curious, Lin waddled closer and saw that they were building a spaceship.

"Hey — why are you guys building a spaceship? Are you astronauts?" Lin asked.

Pip looked up from his work and replied, "Not yet, but we're going to be. We are going to be the first penguins ever to launch into space and land on the sun."

"The sun?!" Lin gasped. "But won't the ship burn up?"

Pip chuckled. "No," he said. "We're going to go at night."

Q: Why did the two penguins fight with the Club Penguin Clock Tower?

A: Because the clock struck one.

Q: Where did the hiking penguin rest when he got tired?

A: In his nap-sack.

Q: Why did the silly penguin like working at the clock factory?

A: He liked making faces.

Q: How does a penguin build a house?

A: Igloos it together.

EVE: Is your cough better?

JAN: Much better. I've been practising for weeks.

JEN: I can walk through igloo walls.

KEN: Really? How?

JEN: I use the door.

CAL: Can I hear the joke about the five metre wall around the snow fort?

DAN: Nope.

CAL: Why?

DAN: Because you'll never get over it.

In the Book Room

Notice: The following books are _not_ available in the Book Room:

All About Ice Fishing

by Howie Ketchum

Music Appreciation

by Phil Harmonic

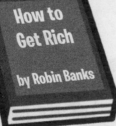

How to Get Rich

by Robin Banks

Making an Igloo

by Bill Dean Blocks

Outdoor Cooking

by Barbara Q. Grill

Q: Who's the head of the penguin navy?

A: Admiral Byrd.

Q: What kind of bird can write underwater?

A: A ballpoint penguin.

Q: Why are penguins so popular on the Internet?

A: Because they have Web feet.

Q: What did the penguin say to the librarian after leaving his books out in the rain?

A: Sorry, my books are over-dew.

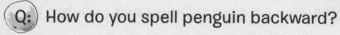

Q: How do you spell penguin backward?

A: P-E-N-G-U-I-N B-A-C-K-W-A-R-D.

Q: What did the penguin say when he stubbed his toe on the sofa?

A: C-ouch.

Q: What letter can a penguin sail on?

A: The C.

ELI: I got an *F* on my test because I couldn't remember where the South Pole was.

FAY: Next time, remember where you put things.

GUS: My wing's asleep.

HAL: I'll talk very quietly.

Q: A penguin knocked over his cup in the Book Room, getting the *mancala* table all wet, yet there was not a drop of hot chocolate in sight. How is this possible?

A: The glass was filled with tea.

Coffee Talk at the Coffee Shop

Sam was enjoying a cup of tea in the Coffee Shop when he noticed a familiar face at the next table. He gathered up his courage and asked, "Excuse me, but aren't you Penelope Fitzwater, star of the new show at The Stage?"

"Yes, I am," she acknowledged, and graciously signed an autograph for Sam.

Sam went over to his friend, Pip, a waiter, who was busy clearing off a table. "Do you know you have Fitzwater in the house?" Sam asked.

"I'm not sure about that," Pip replied. "But we do have hot chocolate and coffee at the counter."

Q: How do penguins mix liquids in science class?

A: With beak-ers.

Q: What are two things a penguin cannot eat for breakfast?

A: Lunch and dinner.

Q: What do penguins eat for breakfast?

A: Ice Cream of Wheat.

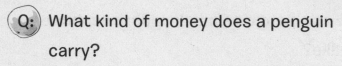 **Q:** What kind of money does a penguin carry?

A: Cold cash.

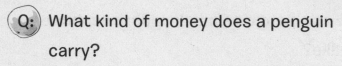 **Q:** Why did the penguin smile at the banana?

A: Because he found it a-peel-ing.

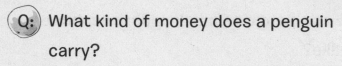 **Q:** What shouldn't a penguin drink when it has a cold?

A: Cough-ee.

Q: What sound do Club Penguin telephones make?

A: *Wing, wing.*

KAY: Help me fix a cup of hot chocolate.

LEN: Why? Is it broken?

MAE: This tea tastes funny.

NAN: Then why aren't you laughing?

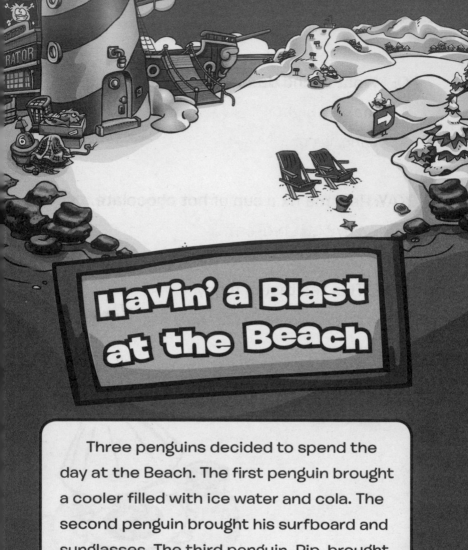

Havin' a Blast at the Beach

Three penguins decided to spend the day at the Beach. The first penguin brought a cooler filled with ice water and cola. The second penguin brought his surfboard and sunglasses. The third penguin, Pip, brought a car door.

"What's that for?" Pip's friends asked.

Pip replied, "Well, if it gets too hot, I can roll down the window."

Q: What kind of fish do penguins catch at night?

A: Starfish.

Q: Why didn't the penguin wash himself after he went to the Beach?

A: Because he was a sunbather.

Q: What does a penguin get when it eats gumdrops at the Beach?

A: Sandy candy.

Q: What washes up on tiny seashores?

A: Microwaves.

Q: What does a penguin wear to the Beach?

A: An iced T-shirt.

Q: Why didn't the penguin go to the Beach with his friends?

A: He was feeling under the feather.

Q: What do you call a penguin in the desert?

A: Lost.

PIP: Knock, knock.

RAE: Who's there?

PIP: Justin.

RAE: Justin who?

PIP: Justin time for some swimming!

Laughing at the Lighthouse

Pip called in sick to work at the Lighthouse one morning. Pip's friend Kip stopped by his house to see how he was doing.

"You gotta help me, Kip," Pip said. "When I press my forehead with my wing, it really hurts. And when I do the same to my cheek, it's also painful. Even if I press on my tummy, I cry out. What can it be?"

Kip looked at Pip for a few seconds and quickly came up with the answer. "You have a broken wing."

Q: How did the sea greet the iceberg?

A: It waved.

Q: Who gets up earlier: a penguin who works at a lighthouse or a duck who works at a lighthouse?

A: The duck. He gets up at the quack of dawn.

Q: Can a penguin jump higher than the Lighthouse?

A: Yes. Lighthouses can't jump.

Q: Where's the best place to be if there's a hurricane in the South Pole?

A: The North Pole.

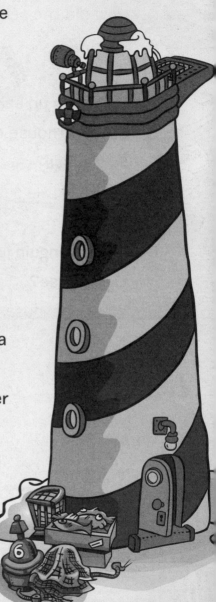

UMA: I bet I can drop this snowball 12 metres from the top of the Lighthouse without breaking it.

VIV: How is that possible?

UMA: Climb to the top of a 15 metre-high lighthouse and drop the snowball over the edge. For the first 12 metres, it won't break.

Down at the Dock

Kip called the Hydro-Hopper driver on the telephone one afternoon and asked, "May I speak with Mr or Mrs Anchors please?" The driver said, "I'll check if they're here — hold on."

The driver walked up and down the Dock, asking all the penguins if they were named Mr Anchors or Mrs Anchors. After a few minutes, he returned to the phone and said, "No, I'm sorry, there are no Anchors here."

Kip responded, "Then how do you keep your boats from drifting away?"

Q: What do your buddies say to you before you play *Jet Pack Adventure*?

A: Beak careful out there.

Q: What did the boat say when it came to shore?

A: What's up, Dock?

Q: What lies at the bottom of the sea and shakes?

A: A nervous wreck.

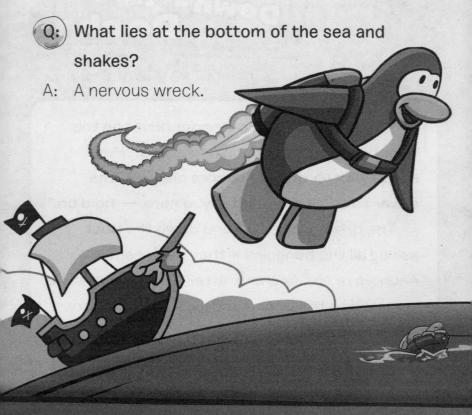

These days, deciding what to wear out, simply wears you out!

Because he was
standing on the deck!

Q: What is something Rockhopper never wants to see on his ship?

A: A sink.

Q: What holds water even though it's full of holes?

A: A sponge.

Q: What did the penguin call his favourite relative, the boat mechanic?

A: Auntie Freeze.

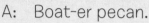 **Q:** What kind of ice cream does
a sailor penguin like?

A: Boat-er pecan.

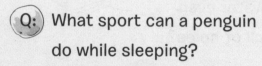 **Q:** What sport can a penguin
do while sleeping?

A: Snore-keling.

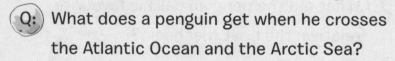 **Q:** What does a penguin get when he crosses
the Atlantic Ocean and the Arctic Sea?

A: A bigger boat.

Overheard at the Plaza

Pip came running up to a Rescue Squad penguin. He said, "My friend has been hit on the head by his boomerang."

The Rescue Squad penguin nodded and said, "I know which penguin you are talking about. I saw him playing with his boomerang earlier and thought someone might get hurt. I told him to throw that boomerang away."

Pip said, "He did . . . but it came back."

Q: What's black and white and goes around and around?

A: A penguin in a revolving door.

Q: What did the lawyer penguin wear to court?

A: A law-suit.

BEN: Why are you wearing my new raincoat without asking?

CY: Because I didn't want to get your new T-shirt wet.

DON: I know a place in town where we can eat dirt cheap.

GIL: Yuck. Why would I want to eat dirt?

Q: What do you call it when a penguin accidentally bumps into a bell?

A: A wing ding.

Q: How did the penguin leave his band?

A: On a sour note.

Getting Silly at the Ski Village

Pip and his friend Kip decided to hike across the island and go on an ice-fishing trip. Once they got there, they rented a boat and bought new fishing rods and bait. It cost them 4,000 coins! At the end of their trip, all they had caught was one small fish.

"Aw shucks," Kip said. "Do you realize we spent about 2,000 coins each to catch this one fish?"

"Wow," replied Pip. "At that rate, it's a good thing we only caught one."

Q: Why is it so easy to weigh fish?

A: Because they have their own scales.

Q: What's the best way to catch a fish?

A: Have someone throw it to you.

Q: How does a penguin communicate with a fish?

A: He drops him a line.

Q: What do you call a fish with no eyes?

A: A fsh.

Q: What musical instrument can a penguin use to catch fish?

A: A clari-net.

Q: What's the penguin fisherman's favourite baseball position?

A: Catcher.

Q: What is black and white, black and white, black and white and black and white?

A: A penguin rolling down a hill.

Q: What do you call a pretty penguin who goes skiing?

A: Sloping Beauty.

Q: What kind of bug loves the snow?

A: The mo-ski-to.

Q: Why didn't the penguins have fun on the ski trip?

A: Because they were snow-bored-ing.

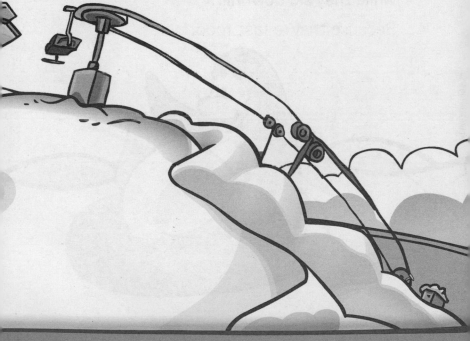

Q: How do you find out what the weather is like on top of a mountain?

A: You climate.

Q: What's black and white and goes up and down?

A: A penguin stuck on a chairlift.

Q: Why do penguins like to eat french fries while they ski downhill?

A: Because they're fast food.

JAN: Will this path take me down the mountain?

JEN: No, you'll have to ski there.

MEL: I really needed this ski holiday from my job sharpening pizza cutters.

SUE: How come?

MEL: I find everything much too dull.

STU: Can I hear the joke about the chairlift?

TY: Nope.

STU: Why?

TY: Because it's over your head.

Pip didn't know much about sports, but when his friends invited him to watch a hockey game at the Ice Rink, he agreed enthusiastically. After one of the players scored, the crowd screamed and one excited penguin held up a giant sign that read, "G O A L !" After cheering wildly, Pip asked, "Who's Al?"

Q: Why don't puffles like to skate at the Ice Rink?

A: Because it's for the birds.

Q: Why did the penguin cross the Ice Rink?

A: To get to the other slide.

Q: What does a penguin get when he crosses karate moves with hockey sticks?

A: Chopsticks.

Q: What do you call a pretty penguin who falls on the ice?

A: Slipping Beauty.

VIV: Are you meeting your friend at the skating rink?

ANN: No, I've known him for years.

Party at the Pizza Parlor

Pip got a job as host at the Pizza Parlor. One day, a penguin called to make reservations.

"Could we have a table for four at 7:00 ?" the penguin asked.

"I'm sorry," Pip answered, "but we're all booked for that time. We could seat you at 6:45, though. Will that be okay?"

The penguin accepted 6:45 and made the reservation.

"OK," Pip confirmed. "Just be advised that you may have to wait 15 minutes for your table."

ELI: Why is my pizza smashed?

FAY: You told me to make you a pizza and step on it.

Q: **What did the penguin say to the pizza?**

A: Nice to eat you.

Q: **Does a penguin like to eat all the pizza you give him?**

A: No, he likes to pick and chews.

Q: What do penguins like to eat with their pizza?

A: Cold slaw.

Q: What do some penguins like to have for lunch?

A: Icebergers.

Q: What's in a penguin's favourite salad?

A: Iceberg lettuce.

Q: How does a penguin make pancakes?

A: With its flippers.

Q: What does a penguin say after eating a huge dinner?

A: BURP.

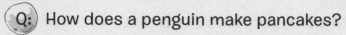

Q: What does a lumberjack penguin like on his pizza?

A: Pine-apple.

Q: Why should a penguin's dinner table have four equal sides?

A: So he can eat a square meal.

Q: Why did the penguin go on a diet?

A: He wanted a new weigh of life.

Q: What do penguins sing on a birthday?

A: "Freeze a jolly good fellow."

YIP: There's a race in the kitchen!

NIP: What's happening?

YIP: The lettuce is a head, the water is running and the tomato is trying to ketchup!

ART: I'm tired of making pizza. Can't we make a jelly roll instead?

ALF: How do you make a jelly roll?

ART: You push it down a hill.

BEN: Did you hear what happened to the penguin who broke into the Pizza Parlor?

DAN: Yeah. He got arrested for disturbing the pizza.

Playing at the Pet Shop

When Pip's friend Lin was getting ready for a party in her igloo one day, she asked Pip to come over and help her take care of her puffle, Boo-Boo. Pip, who was anxious to help his friend, agreed and asked, "What should I feed Boo-Boo for lunch?"

"There's all kinds of puffle food in the kitchen," Lin replied. "Why don't you decide for yourself? In fact, just pretend I'm not home."

A few minutes later, her mobile phone rang. "Hello?" she answered. On the other end, she heard Pip's voice. "Hi, Lin, um . . . what should I feed Boo-Boo for lunch?"

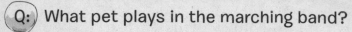

Q: What pet plays in the marching band?

A: The trum-pet.

Q: What is a puffle's favourite game to play with a penguin?

A: Beak-a-boo.

GUS: It's a good thing you named your puffle Ginger.

GIL: Why?

GUS: Because that's what everyone keeps calling it.

HAL: Where are you going?

IRA: I'm going to buy some new sunglasses and a puffleway.

HAL: What's a puffleway?

IRA: Anywhere from 5 kg to 10 kg.

Forest Fun

Pip went hiking through the Forest with his friend Kip. Pip brought along a thermos. Kip had never seen one and asked what it was.

"It's a thermos," replied Pip. "The guy at the Sport Shop told me it's used for keeping hot things hot and cold things cold."

"Sounds great," said Kip. "What do you have in it?"

"Hot chocolate and ice cream."

Q: How does a tree get a fresh start?

A: It turns over a new leaf.

Q: What did the penguin say when he held a branch above his head?

A: This is a stick-up.

Q: What kind of tree is good at maths?

A: A geome-tree.

Q: What did the tree say to the penguin with the rake?

A: Leaf me alone.

ANNE: That sure is an angry-looking tree.

NAN: Don't worry, its bark is worse than its bite.

LEN: Knock, knock.

KEN: Who's there?

LEN: Little old lady.

KEN: Little old lady who?

LEN: Ooh, you're a good yodeler.

Busting a Move at the Night Club

Pip went into the Night Club to dance for a while. Then he went upstairs to play video games, eat some peanuts and make some new friends. As he sat down to drink his cola, he heard a tiny voice say, "I like your hat!" Pip looked all around him but couldn't see where the voice came from. A minute later he heard the same voice saying, "Cool sweatshirt!" Pip was really puzzled. He asked a penguin next to him if he heard the voice, too.

The penguin replied, "It's the peanuts — they're complimentary."

Q: Where do penguins go to dance?

A: The Snow Ball.

Q: What's a singing penguin's favourite drink?

A: Cola-la-la-la.

Q: How can a penguin make a dance floor bigger?

A: When he steps onto it, he adds two feet.

Q: What is a penguin's favourite party game?

A: Sardines.

JOE: May I see you pretty soon?

MAE: I think I'm pretty now, thank you very much!

NAN: Knock, knock.

PIP: Who's there?

NAN: Norma Lee.

PIP: Norma Lee who?

NAN: Norma Lee I stay in my igloo and read on Friday nights, but tonight I wanna boogie!

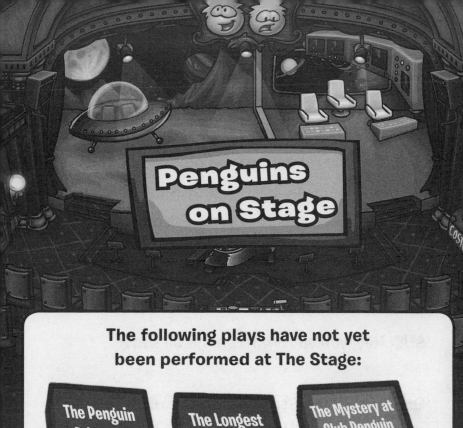

The following plays have not yet been performed at The Stage:

The Penguin Prisoners

by Frida Birds

The Longest Play

by Adeline N. Adanuther

The Mystery at Club Penguin

by Butler Diddit

The Punctual Penguin

by Justin Tyme

The Solitary Penguin

I. Malone

Playing Hide and Seek

by I.C. Hugh

SUE: Will you remember me tomorrow?

TOM: Of course I will.

SUE: Will you remember me next week?

TOM: Yes.

SUE: Will you remember me next month?

TOM: I promise I will always remember you.

SUE: Knock, knock.

TOM: Who's there?

SUE: Hey, you've forgotten me already!

Q: **What is The Stage made out of?**

A: Wooden you like to know?

Q: **What did the penguin do when he forgot his lines in the play?**

A: He winged it.

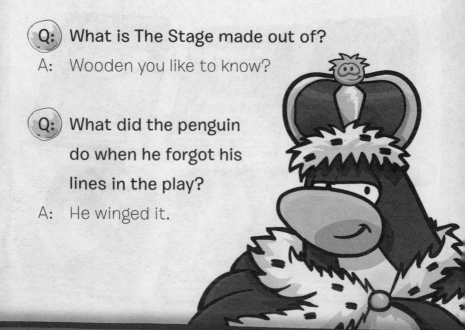

VIV: I want to sing solo in the play.

TED: OK, but make sure you don't sing so low that no one can hear you.

UMA: I want my voice to fill the entire auditorium.

JED: OK, but make sure you leave some room for the audience.

BOB: Why didn't you stay for the second act of the play last night?

AMY: Because the programme said it took place five years later.

TAD: Before I got this job at The Stage, I worked for the circus. I was the penguin cannonball and got shot out of a cannon.

ADA: How was it?

TAD: It wasn't so good. I got fired all the time.